The Musings of a Crazy Cat lady in the Dark

By Valerie Fabian

THE MUSINGS OF A CRAZY CAT LADY IN THE DARK

First edition. September 1, 2024.

ISBN: 979-8227233585

Written by valerie fabian.

Table of Contents

For my beautiful family and friends, for helping me have the courage to bring my poetry to life.

And for poets past and present, thank you for all of the words that speak directly to our souls.

To Be Read

So many books
so little time
the 'To Be Read' pile
ever growing.

Soon as tall as the tree
that made the books
standing like a proud parent
basking in the words of glory.

Stories, novels, tales, poems.
All of the words,
wanting to be let out,
wanting to be released.

Sit still.
Relax.
Breathe.
Escape into this new world.

Wishes from the Stars

It is all written in the dreams
that you throw out
into the night skies,
like wishes from the stars,
if you desire them hard enough
they may even come true.

Love Thyself More

An ecstasy in the sunlight,
a moonbeam on the skin
a love that lights up the world
and draws you further in.

Starlight in the night skies,
a solace for the soul
a piece of heart awakens
a love that will console.

For once and all beholden,
the only love that's true
a perfect glove that fits,
is the love you hold for you.

The Best of Days

A universe of warm sand
sticks from toes to face
grainy reminders
of our favourite place
collecting seashells
along the shore
never enough
always wanting more
donkey rides
ice-cream cones
love and laughter
no mobile phones
building castles
buckets and spades
seashore walks
the best of days.

The Bucket List

Fill your bucket with early morning coffee;
watching the sun rise
with sleepy sunsets
and stolen kisses in the moonlight.

Fill your bucket with good books to read;
and fine wine to drink
as you listen to sweet music
on a lazy summers day or a rainy winters evening.

Fill your bucket with good friends and family;
who fit like a comfortable pair of gloves
or warm fluffy slippers that
you never want to remove.

Fill your bucket with cats or dogs;
or even better with both
and come to know uncomplicated love
in its most loyal and unconditional form.

Fill your bucket with time well spent;
in a beautiful garden or magnificent forest,
a soothing gentle way
to find the peace that you crave.

Fill your bucket with travel and adventures;
to far away exotic places
and enjoy new people and cultures,
but always return to the place that feels like home.

Fill your bucket with memories of smiles;
and dreams of magical days
but most of all remember,
to fill your bucket up with love.

Colours of Dawn and Day

Look up for the magic
of messages in the sky
where the sunsets make love
and take the breath away.

Where light meets the dusk
and dusk becomes the night
an ethereal portrait of beauty
the slate wiped clean and bright.

The sun begins it majestic rise
a future of promise shows the way
beaming over land and spirit
mixing colours of dawn and day.

The Hygge Sanctuary

Find serenity in the simplest pleasures,
This Hygge they all talk about
must have something to it,
friends, family, graciousness,
candles and soft blankets,
sounds pretty cosy
and delectably calm,
a small slice of heaven,
let's make a start there.

In the sweet recesses of the soul
find a sanctuary
that is all yours,
a place to call home,
a place to hide from harm,
a space filled with love,
find your peace,
light the candles,
and all will be well.

A Contented Life

Take me to my happy place,
where waves wash against the shore,
the sunrise sparkles in the morning
and sunsets leave you wanting more.

A garden overflowing with beauty
flowers blooming perfect and bright,
a crowded forest full of noble trees
life noisy but out of sight.

A cosy house with warmth and food
a few crazy mouths to feed,
coffee brewing in a rumbling pot
plenty of books on shelves to read.

A contented life is easily found
in many shapes and spaces,
and the easiest route to happiness
is seeing magic in normal places.

Rocks Skimming Through Summer

Rocks skimming through summer,
sand slipping through perfectly polished feet,
waves of light and sea
bring life back to jagged overworked brains
and worn out, torn bodies.
Put aside the normality
for two weeks of fun in the sun
whilst becoming more undone,
the cares and worries tossed aside,
sapped souls replenished in the salt sprayed air
just beware of the sunbed wars,
a secret contest for all nations on earth,
a fight to the death for a suntan?
You might actually prefer the 9-5!

The Annual Dance

It is already January,
the harsh winds howl
like a rampaging beast
across a desolate city,
bringing with it
a cool winter chill.
Diving into the fresh February air,
which blows through even faster.
The March winds are gentler,
a mixing of cold meeting warm,
leading to April sunshine and showers
that are both new and familiar all at the same time.
The seasons splash through the year,
leading a cheerful spring into
May and a sense of rebirth for us all.
June beckons with sweet delights,
all fresh daisies and blooms budding anew.
Then into July and the fullness of
a rich summer begins,
bringing with it a comforting heat
from the earth.

August brings fond memories
of precious sunny days,
when without a care

we would live a dance of joy,
in the warming rays.
September seems slightly melancholy
in her arrival,
as she starts stripping bare the earth
leading to the mischievousness
of October with all its pranks to play,
as we make our way
into a bleak November,
when sleep is falling upon the earth once again.
December brings with it
a strange poignancy
and new hope,
as the year is nearly over
but getting ready with a twinkle in her eye
to lead us on a merry prance
and complete the never-ending cycle
of the seasons once again.

Sleep On It

Come at it with fresh eyes in the morning,
when a new day is dawning
and life feels calm and light,
the rising sun a magical sight.

Grassy fields glistening full of dew,
and petals of flowers open anew,
birds are singing melodious songs
and flock overhead in murmuring throngs.

The sky a beckoning cyan blue,
a new palette wiped clean just for you,
the world starts to wake in all its glory,
time to write today's story.

Each Sunset a Heartbreak

Sunsets as beautiful as the heavens,
an artist's canvas of dreams,
a reminder of the constant passing of time,
marking the beginning of something
but also, the end.
A heartbreak each cycle,
as day slips away from the light,
and life in each disappearing sunset
gradually gives way to the night.

Sunset Hues

Melodic hues of sunburnt reds
in the fading of the sunset light
gold tipped skies a brilliant sight
colourful cacophonies,
playing silent symphonies
as the day becomes the night.

Catch Us

Shadows cast off
from silent shores,
a whispering in the wind,
a pleading for more,
and in far off distant lands,
a similar raw call,
to please catch us
before we fall.

Atlas of the Heart

The heart holds many roads
mapped by scars woven deep
and well travelled through the years.
The roads lead a merry dance,
some to hell and some to heaven,
some well lit and some well trodden,
the way back home often forgotten.
Some roads lead to pastures new,
a twist a turn, some run uphill.
Some will cross on starry nights
through fields of corn and barley,
taking mystical paths that weave and chart
secret routes to the Atlas of the heart.

Eloquence of Madness

There's a power in the night sky,
a whisper on the breeze,
an eloquence of madness
that brings you to your knees.

Stardust made of liquid
a heart made out of gold,
angels filled with purity,
and magic to behold.

A universe wide open
full of pure mystique,
a god that is forgiving
a love that is unique.

I Can Hear You Dreaming

The midnight hour arrives gently,
the rise and fall of breath,
beauty in far off foreign lands beckons.

The clock keeps ticking,
sleep hits a jagged waters edge,
the cogs of brain cells unwinding.

A transient peace then descends,
between the sleepy veil
of this place and the other.

The passage of time
no longer exists for a moment,
in this secret world between worlds.

But midnight still comes and goes,
the wheels keep turning,
and I can hear you dreaming in your sleep.

Only Cat People Know

Only Cat people know.

Majestic
Regal
Sentient beings
Silently keeping watch over us
as true rulers of the world.
Love must be earned
but once earned the rewards are
marvellous and magical
and sadly unexplainable
to the poor dog people.

Only Dog People Know

Only Dog people know.

Unconditional
Loyal
Love of God
Passed to earth
Love given freely
Angels without wings
but wagging tails instead.
Licks, wags, walks, puppy dog eyes.
Joys unknown for the poor Cat people.

Lucky are the Ones

Lucky,
are the ones with good friends.

Souls that hold you up,
give you hope,
keep you going
support you,
love you,
nourish you,
understand you,
stand by you.

Love,
to all the good friends.

Spice of Life

Don't give up enjoying
whilst you are enduring,
the interesting spices of life.
Each day is a challenge
that is thrown your way,
stay strong hold on tight
perseverance will pay.
This life is for living
take it all in your stride,
eat the cake, drink champagne,
with good friends by your side.

Food for the Soul

You know what's good for the soul?
Those crazy food fuelled nights with close friends,
when the wine flows freely
and the chat never ends.

Where hearts open wide,
dealing with the rawness of life,
and Prosecco takes the edge off
all the trouble and strife.

Where friendly ears listen,
advice is generously told,
a few hugs are given
to help lessen the load.

So, here's to bonds of friendship
and problems that are shared,
a special power between women,
that cannot be compared.

This Parenting Lark

Oh, sweet bundle,
Oh, the joys,
Oh, the terrors,
Oh, the enormity of responsibility.

The sleepless nights
lead to sleepless days,
nappies and poop aplenty.
Playing in the park,
staying up in the dark,
it's not always a joy
this parenting lark.

Not easy for some,
we don't always get it right
but we try,
and then we try again
and we love,
and then we love again
and we give all of our hearts
to this sweet bundle of joy.

All The Love

Families in all shapes,
in all sizes.
Functional
or dysfunctional.
Lessons to be learnt,
lives to be lived.
Disputes to solve,
hugs to be had.
Precious hearts beating,
souls to nourish.
Supportive through the rough times,
joyous through the rest.
From my family to yours,
all the love matters.

Mother Knows Best

Hearts open,
arms always wide.

Love given freely,
with the biggest of smiles.

A treasure beyond measure,
a gift beyond compare.

Preparing 45,000 meals
-or something like that!

Not perfect by any means,
although she always knows best.

A loving guide through life
-until you know best.

Fathers Guiding Hand

A strong brave Bear,
always got your back.
Helping to steer your ship,
as it sails through life.

Omnipresent.
Omnipotent.
Benevolent.
Your own earthly God.

He picks you up
and guides your way,
ever ready to catch
should you fall again.

Rugby Dad.
Football Dad.
Car mad Dad.
Simply the best Dad.

The Moon and Back

We share this brief precious time on earth.
So, I will show you the moon
and the stars
and the endless galaxies to explore.
Your childlike innocence
will look on in wonder
as you ponder your very existence.
I will urge you to follow your dreams
to the moon and back
with my love safely locked in your heart,
and all will be well.

This Girl

Peace
She was a calm gentle soul
a beautiful thinker
with heart spreading wide
a lover of peace and beauty
wanting nothing more
than to daydream
by the warmth of a soothing fire
the girl that you most needed.

Demons
She was a strong passionate soul
with flames at her centre
fighting off relentless demons
with superhuman strength
her courage invincible
mastering her emotions
to become the best possible version of herself
the girl you most admired.

Pure
She was a pure sweet soul
with kindness at her centre
a wisdom beyond her years
a loyal caring friend
with a sparkle in her eyes
and the warmest of spirits
a calmness found in her presence
the girl you most adored.

This Boy

Peace
He was a quiet calm soul
loved his books and computers
the strong silent type
cool as a cucumber
solid as a rock
and dependable too
the boy you most needed.

Demons
He was handsome and debonair
and slightly mischievous
loved to play jokes on you
to keep you on your toes
a kindred spirit with a zest for life
he knew about battling the demons
and could keep you safe
the boy you most admired.

Pure
He was a pure sweet soul
who would do anything for anyone
or go anywhere
a real sports man and great team player
he would always have your back
and support you
the boy you most adored.

Soul Sisters

A pairing of souls,
a twinning of minds,
lives ever intertwined.

A sharing of joys,
a dividing of sorrows,
hearts ever together.

A solving of problems,
a bonding of love,
caring arms holding.

A traversing through life,
a source of support,
Sisters together forever.

Blood Brothers

Bear Cubs.
Pretend fighting.

Football frenzy.
Lego wars.

Nights online.
Gaming joys.

Sweaty armpits.
Smelly socks.

First loves.
Teasing times.

Car rides.
Brothers in arms.

A Mothers Honour

I was chosen,
to bring you into life,
this honour was mine,
my soul's purpose,
and I promised to do my best,
though sometimes it may have been my worst.
A mother's burden,
never light to carry,
for your hearts lie deeply entwined with mine,
for both your joy and your pain
are ever the same as mine,
and a mother is only as happy
as her unhappiest child.

Home Sweet Home

The sweetest of homes
live in the smell
of home baking
and candles lit warmly
on a cold wintry night.

The crumpled bed clothes
and muddy welly boots
piled by the door
often accompanied
by messy wet paw prints.

The scribbled pictures
hanging on fridge doors
multiple toothbrushes
lie side by side
loo paper often hung empty.

The balloons and banners
toys and clothes
come and go through the years
ready to be handed down or
passed on to more needy.

The beans on toast suppers
dens made with blankets
laundry baskets grow daily
and ironing piles
grow even faster.

The migration begins
when one by one they dip a toe
into pastures new
following their own
tentative dreams.

The chaos you will miss
when they fly the nest
just keep the door and arms wide open
for birds always remember
their fastest way home.

Try Again

As we get older,
we feel the sands of time
slipping faster through our grasp.
The tendrils leave behind a glimmer of our lives
that flashed by in less than a moment.
A mere speck in the stardust,
as the aura of the universe surrounds us in its clasp.
Can we atone for our sins
in another place;
can we find an eternity
where time has no meaning
and we get the chance to try again?

World Filled with Love

In the valley of lonely veins,
there is a call for lost souls
that are hungry for flames,
fireflies dance at midnight
under moonlit starry skies
and we find a strange freedom
in cutting lose all the ties
drops of tentative dreams
can be sensed from above
telling us home is where the heart is
and a world filled with love.

Heatwave

It was the hottest day of the summer
and the world was feeling heavy and jaded
a blanket of stars adorned the parched red sky
and somewhere between reality and dreams
the heavens suddenly opened
and drenched us with sweet nectar rain.

Traffic Jams

The joy of traffic jams,
sat waiting in lines,
how much time wasted,
in these anxious confines.
No amount of coffee
can help us change gears,
car rage upon us,
steam pouring from ears.
The seconds turn to minutes,
the minutes turn to hours,
hands tap with frustration,
traffic is out of our powers.
One thing to console you
is that things could be worse,
as getting a puncture,
would be the final curse!

Money Trap

Don't be bequeathed to the money.
Don't be tempted by the sweetness it teases
and that which you crave.

Don't be beholden to the honey
that is purely man made,
designed to hold you tightly in its trap.

Rise above the gloomy skies,
to find the pot of love beyond the rainbows edge,
that you really should desire.

A Love of its Own

Sometimes love is found,
So intense.
So passionate.
So all consuming.
A law of its own.

Sometimes love is lost,
Flames dimming.
A sadness.
A yearning.
A death of its own.

Sometimes love is found again,
Reborn.
Anew.
Everlasting.
A life of its own.

In the Little Things

It's in the little things,
you find the joy.
It's in the little things,
you find the hope.
It's in the little things,
you find the love.
It's in the little things,
you find your people.
It's in the little things,
you find the big things.

Flight of Happiness

Oh, fleeting Happiness,
found in the sweet moments
invisible to the naked eye.

Flights of fancy
and swift with love and desire,
for a happy ever after ending.

Take it when you can,
grab it with all your might,
feast on it and savour the delight.

Happiness flies faster than time can count
so hold onto it tightly,
and fill your life wisely.

School of Thought

Is school a fun place to learn,
or a prison?
Children cooped up like hens,
would they prefer to run free?
Let's look at division
and some more revision.
In Maths learn the price to pay,
in English write some poetry.
Opening of some minds
and the closing of others.
Igniting a joy of learning,
or being put off for life.
Should we stand for it?
or stand against it?
The School of Thought.

A World of Two Halves

A world of two halves.
A strange place to be.

Half the world greedy.
Half the world starving.

Half the world with plenty.
Half the world with nothing.

Half the world living.
Half the world dying.

A world of two halves,
that should become one.

To Do Lists

To Do Lists.

Always
getting longer
getting shorter
more urgent
or less urgent
multiplying
and dividing
with Apps to keep you on track
find the ideal work-life balance hack.

The problem is,
is life done once they are?

The Wheel Keeps Turning

Work to live
or live to work.
The emails come
in a never ending stream,
of ready made swamp
for the mind.
The relentless phone calls
set your teeth on edge,
the complaints
from customers
growing daily.
No rest for the wicked,
just countless bills to pay
the world becoming
a harsh place,
with no respite
just a race to the finish
and the hamster wheel
keeps on turning,
as we die to work
and work to die.

The Social Media Conundrum

False.
Perfect.
Imperfect beauty with no flaws.

Lies.
Truths.
Tangled webs and Tik Tok dances.

Human Ego.
Revered,
or destroyed by the masses?

Empty Room

The hollowness
is all consuming
no comfy chair
to rest your weary bones
just a throb of emptiness
filling the vast space
leaving a trail
of sadness
like crumbs to follow
though nothing is there
just an invisible room
with no windows
and no hope
as you lay bare your soul
naked for all to see.

Give Ourselves Grace

Searching out castles in the sky,
full of lucid dreams
as we find our way,
in this journey we call life.

A journey full of joy and pain
both for ourselves and others,
no easy straight line to follow
just all the ups and downs.

When dealing with more
tortured souls than our own,
give ourselves grace to listen,
for one day we may gain our angel wings.

Residue

The residue of lonely nights
praying for more
and wanting more
remains a reminder of those darker times.

When life seemed barren
and incomplete
the light at the end of the tunnel
was just out of reach.

But with small steps forward
and little by little
you moved away from the ledge
that was holding you back.

Feeling stronger, feeling braver
to go find your best life
the idea of living
finally outweighing the idea of leaving.

I Found it in Me

I found it in me
the soul of a warrior.

To live or not to live
to die or not to die.

The flames of passion, once burned,
now embers.

But the life in me flickers still.
I will not go.

I am brave.
I am ready.
I will live.

Luminosity

In your darkest hour
when all seems lost,
you find a hidden strength
and we see you
lighten the dark,
with joyful luminosity,
as your smile lights up
the whole room.

Silent Strength

Where is the real strength?

Is it in the mother who is coping
or the one throwing it all away.
Is it in the tough guy at the gym
or teenager trying not to die.
Is it in the builder, building houses
or the priest praying for lost souls.
Is it in the soldier shooting the enemy
or the surgeon repairing the bones.
Is it in the people getting it all right
or the ones getting it all wrong.
Is it in all of us in some small silent way?

Doing our best to stay strong.

The Road to Repair

The demons fight their way
through to you,
no mountain too big or too tall,
guard carefully your weary heart
and watch out for the void in your soul.

The night eats the noise
of the spinning world,
repelling the probing forces,
deafening in the silence,
as good versus evil discourses.

Your indomitable spirit
has a hidden strength
to release the shackles of despair,
step outside of the shadows,
and start on the road to repair.

I Believe in You

I see you full of doubts and fear
your worries poison in your ear,
if only you'd believe,
like I believe in you,
then all your dreams and wishes
would wonderfully come true.

Continuum of Reality

Do you often feel,
life is cut,
into mere chunks of time,
that grow ever smaller,
diminishing with age.

We must savour every minute,
every second,
of this fast paced life,
that slices through
our threescore years and ten.

A mere scar in the never-ending
continuum of reality.
Our light shone,
for just the tiniest of moments
in the blink of an eye.

Did it mean anything
or nothing at all?

The Power of Words

It is in the power of words,
a person can be lifted or destroyed
in the warmth of tender prose
or daggers of cruelty piercing the heart.

It is in the power of words,
a person can fall in or out of love
in the caress of a silky whisper,
or the bitter coldness of abuse.

It is in the power of words,
a person can heal or die,
be lifted from the darkness
or sadly left to decay.

It is in the power of words,
you must take care
for you have a dangerous power
of which to be aware.

The Floods of War

The ticking of the silent bombs
floods your ears.
The sight of men against men
floods your eyes.
The pouring of the blood red blood
floods your hands.
The dulling of the senses
floods your brain.
The killing of the innocent
floods your heart.

Senseless.
Ruthless.
Killing machines.
Man.

Beacons of Light

Tears fall from lonely clouds
in the twilight hours
between life and death,
hearts covered in hurt
and minds seeking solace,
looking to find answers
from those who see things
others cannot.
The beautiful souls
that are made of pure love
and help lead us away
from pain and despair,
our shining beacons of light
in the healing stardust.

To the Lost

Always searching,
lost souls.
Always hurting.
Always hiding.

Always tortured,
lost souls.
Always thinking.
Always wondering.

Always needing,
lost souls.
Always feeling.
Always loving.

Do not worry,
lost souls,
for you are never alone.

The Dying of the Light

To what depth of magnitude
can sorrow and despair lead
should we hasten to quiet the racing mind
and quench the pounding heartbeat
or should we just let it wash over us gently
until equilibrium is found again
in the silence of the mind
in the solitude of the heart
we will find peace once more
in the dying of the light.

Battle wounds

The scars remind you
of battles well fought,
in a life well lived.
Of wounds once opened,
now healed.
Of torment that once
ripped you apart
at the seams,
that now lies quietly
and somewhere dormant
like a sleeping volcano,
no longer a source of fire,
just a constant dull ache,
rumbling away in the background,
in the grand scheme of living,
through the constant wars of life.

Life and Death

The words come and go
they speak of truth
and of beauty
they speak of life
and death
and cruelty
to find a meaning
and a purpose
to all this insanity
impossible questions
unfathomable answers
for our soul's reality.

In Amongst the Chaos

In amongst the chaos
of the normal days
of the busiest days
of the pointless days.

In amongst the chaos
of the happiest days
of the saddest days
of the difficult days.

In amongst the chaos
of the joyful days
of the darkest days
of the endless days.

I hope you find some peace.

Dance Away the Storms

The sweet sweat pours,
the feet tingle,
the blood boils,
passionate and frenzied, like a tornado.

Tango, Tango,
swirling, twirling.

The sweet hips sway,
the back arches,
the hands weave away,
sensual and luxurious, like a whirlwind.

Mambo, Mambo,
swirling, twirling.

The sweet limbs flow,
the heart pounds,
the lungs roar,
powerful and destructive, like a hurricane.

Rumba, Rumba
swirling, twirling.
Dance pretty lady,
Dance those storms away.

Assassins of Happiness

Like thieves in the night,
be aware of the assassins of happiness,
that fly in
on the back of anxiety.

To steal your calm,
to swipe your joy
to seize your hope
and savour your very essence.

As cunning as a fox
and stealthy as a tiger,
in the darkness of the night,
the assassins will come.

So steel your resolve,
dear brave heart,
and seal your precious soul,
dear strong heart.
For the assassins are not welcome here.

Cascade

Cascades of beauty
pointless to non-seeing eyes
realising time is cruel
and youth is often
wasted on the young
we are all locked in gilded cages
where everyone is different
but everyone is exactly the same
and usually the quietest of people
have the loudest of minds
so value your peace
turn off the noise of the world
put the phones down
and let us find our way
back to each other
in this fleeting of lives.

The Key

Positivity is the treasured key,
to opening all locks.

The lock to your beautiful mind
to your precious heart,
to your lifelong dreams,
to your cherished soul.

Push through the door with all your might
to get through to the other side
where joy awaits you and knows no bounds
where sunlight filters through the rainbows
and shadows are left dissolving in despair
freed from the chains holding you back
no longer trapped there
you now have the key.

Moonlight Serenade

The moonlight plays a secret serenade,
as it watches longingly over star crossed lovers.
Light me up in the moons gleam,
so that I may walk proudly out of the shadows,
with fear no longer holding me back,
I will find strength in the moonlight's powers.

Ageless

The ageless ones,
live quietly amongst us,
they don't need to be loud
to just sit and ponder
upon the ways of the world.
They are there to guide us
in mysterious ways,
wiser and kinder,
than the entire human race.
We can gain countenance
from their pureness of grace.

Persevere

It is in the peace and quiet
our heartbeats are often the loudest,
and our minds have the power
to see the good or the bad,
but with strength we can try to persevere
and let peace finally reign in our land.

The Life Within

Souls on fire,
souls alive,
flames burning bright,
life seems easy for some.

Souls struggling,
souls withering,
flames burning low,
life too hard for some.

Souls searching,
souls releasing,
flames simmering,
life worth trying again,

Souls reconnecting,
souls healing,
flames reigniting,
life for living again.

A Strange Peace

There is a strange peace to be had,
in the twilight hours,
with nothing but your own
thoughts for company.

A delve into your very soul,
to find out who you are
and what you want,
the innermost secrets you desire.

The voices come,
sometimes loud, sometimes quiet,
not always friendly,
but still a part of your hive being.

If you listen very carefully,
you will hear them speak what is true,
that if you dream hard enough,
the next big thing is you.

You are Home

Rest your head weary one,
for you are home now.
No fights to win,
no relentless stress
to overcome
just loving arms
to keep you safe
from the harm of the
often cruel world.

Find your peace dear one,
replenish the spirit
and the inner strength
will come bubbling to the surface
ready for you
to spread your wings
and face the outside world
with a courageous heart
once again tomorrow.

Sweet Soul

On days like today
sweet soul,
let no one tell you
that you are anything but beautiful.

You have a quiet strength
that comes from the battles
you have fought
and won over.

You are a mighty warrior
with the gentleness of an angel
and everything you touch
will turn to grace and hope.

You are a shining light
with a bright future ahead
that is all yours
for the taking.

Brave Soldier

My dearest friend
as brave as the soldiers
facing wars
though it was no mortal enemy
you had to face
but death itself
who squared up to you
and you fought him off bravely
and fortunately won
where others heartbreakingly lost
similar battles before you
so you must live on courageously
and follow your dreams
with a host of angels
residing in your pocket.

Angel Breath

Take a sweet breath dear soul,
for you are whole and pure
and a glorious miracle of pulsing veins and tendons
that keep you alive and kicking.
Our heartbeats each have a unique countdown
of this precious time we are given,
so be sure to make each minute matter,
until you take your last angel breath.

Give Me

Give me the wings of a butterfly,
so that I might dance in the air
and please you with my beauty.
Give me the song of the nightingale.
So that I might captivate you
with my beautiful melodies.
Give me the nectar of the honeybee,
So that I might tempt you
with my sweetness.
Give me the strength of a lioness
So that I might impress you
with my bravery.
Give me more of myself.

Hope

Blossoms dance on cherry trees,
dreams drift in on the breeze,
blankets of clouds tell a story in the night sky.
Hold onto your hope when all else fails
and swallow the guilty pride
that is holding you back,
let destiny pull you forwards
to the where the starlight lives.

Bright Moon

In the jet black darkness,
the bright moon shows its face,
a double sided conundrum
full of mystery and grace.

Half moon, full moon, blood moon,
a shining and potent essence,
an imposing majestic entity,
reminds the earth of its presence.

Guarding over the night sky,
enticing lovers never to part,
the beauty of the silent moon
a total eclipse of the heart.

The Silent Forest

The silent forest awakens
a hushed stillness as it starts to breathe.
Mist swirls through the giant redwoods
like ghosts of ancestor's past.

Squirrels busily scampering,
gathering what foods they can.
Deer's invisible to the eyes,
grace the forest with a royal command.

The mighty roots hold steadfast,
leaves whisper a special song,
branches like majestic entities,
guarding over the sacred land.

The Sands of Time

The sands of time
weave a magical web around us,
leaving echoes of our youth.
Little do we understand when five years old
and life seems full
of wonder, colour and mystery.
And suddenly the minutes have ticked by,
and we are over fifty
and life seems slightly tinged with grey.
Where did the time fly?
Is it somewhere tangible
or in another space.
Drifting through the Universe,
the inky blackness holds no clocks,
just an infinite and everlasting darkness.

Somehow, we are both alive and dead at the same time.

Infinite Universe

Universe so infinite,
so impossible to understand,
our tiny human brains,
cannot begin to comprehend,
the mysteries it holds.

Full of chemistry and physics,
astronomy and strange magic.
Stars, sands, particles, planets,
even perhaps,
angels and heaven?

Stardust

Living on borrowed time
is what they say
more poignant as you lay deep
in the middle ages.
Trying to live best
a life well lived
is it pre-ordained
when we will meet our deaths?
Looking up at the stars
how long they have lived
an infinite millennial lives
compared to us.
Centuries and eons flown past
a countless souls
come and gone
to stardust.
Was it ever enough?

Reverie

She was a calm
and gentle breeze,
a blissful reverie,
whispering in the midnight forest.
She gave herself permission to fly
but would always return home
and find her sanctuary
by the warmth of a quiet fireside
a peaceful daydream
to reside inside her head.

The Millpond of Life

A sense of calmness descends
upon the millpond of life,
writing an unseen story
where we can hide away from the injustices of the world.
Putting evil to one side for a heartbeat,
to try and see just the good,
in the multi-faceted faces of the human existence,
a place where all is well and no terror lives,
-it can only really be heaven.

Timeless

A distant star explodes
and a universe of sand
falls timeless through our hands,
ahead, behind, before,
with an eternity to explore

Angel One

A soul who is kind,
wiser than most.

Hands in mine,
hearts ever melded.

Spreading her wings,
ready to fly

A fellow traveller,
along the road of kindness.

I could not do life
without you by my side.

Freckles

Freckles of beauty
shine on cheeks with grace,
a soul filled with stars
that show on your face.

Little Dove

Little lost soul,
traversing life alone,
no mum, no dad, no love.

Sent to me like a little Dove,
wings hurting,
needs nurturing.

Pushing away all who help,
hang on, don't give up,
show the way for little Dove.

One day,
she may find a way,
to accept the love.

Ripples

Fortune rarely favours the few,
fighting silent battles,
painful hearts crying,
for a future of missing you.

Watching loved ones struggle,
knowing life will never be the same,
when you slip away
into that forbidden place.

Leaving us numb,
with a hole that will never fill,
a chasm so deep,
in the never ending precipice of life.

A loss felt so deeply
it sends out vast ripples of tears
into the universe
for a person well loved.

The Pain

When I write
the words whisper loudly
too beautiful to ignore
an anthem of songbirds
singing on the page
the letters released
no longer locked in a cage
but ready for sharing
and wisdom gained
an elegant prose
speaks its tale
for there is life in the words
and they will prevail
joy follows sorrow
tears follow the rain
peace follows loss
without any gain
and in the loving
is the knowing
nothing will be the same
for there is no real life
without any pain.

Waves of Grief

It comes in waves; the grief,
It comes in waves; the pain,
It comes in waves the losing you,
until it comes again.

It moves in waves; the sorrow,
It moves in waves; the loss,
It moves in waves remembering you,
until we meet again.

It speaks in waves; the hurt,
It speaks in waves; the love,
It speaks in waves the missing you,
until we speak again.

You

You are gone.
In another place,
another dimension,
separated by time and space
a billion light years away
or just next door?

For All Eternity

I feel you,
near but far
I hear you,
loud but silent
I see you,
there but nowhere
I miss you,
here and now
I love you,
for all eternity.

Tangled Threads

The tangled threads of grief
leave heartstrings forever tugging,
as sorrow weaves it way around our souls.
Knitting the pain of loss together,
with tendrils of unspoken love,
the knots of hurt in our stomachs bind tightly,
sadness intertwined with poignant memories
weave a bittersweet taste in our minds.
The day that we lost you
is now eternally etched
into the fibre of our beings forever.

A Whisper

As close as a whisper
as far away as the stars
a love never ending,
you will always be ours.
Up high in the heavens
or just the room next door,
where your soul now resides
our love will still pour.
Like the tears on our pillows
blood running through our veins,
in our hearts and minds
your memory remains.

Sunflowers

Every year the sunflowers bloom,
resplendent beauty shining through,
all yellow and golden
majestic and true,
standing proudly in fields
jostling for space,
beautiful faces
to the sky they raise,
to catch sublime pieces
of the reviving sun's rays
and under dazzling skies
of azure blue,
their sunny smiles
make me think of you.

Dragonfly

Delicately divine Dragonfly,
bringer of light, wisdom and transformation.
You light up the world with your pure beauty,
pirouetting sublimely across the lily pads,
dancing elegantly, living life fully.
An ethereal being full of grace,
a ghost of ancestor's past,
forever crossing our paths,
in an eternal ballet of love.

Rainbow Bridge

Over the Rainbow Bridge,
is a beautiful magical place,
full of more love,
than anyone can possibly know.

It holds our pets safe,
until we meet once more,
to smell that sweet paw perfume,
we missed so much.

In this peaceful mystical land,
they will turn to us when we arrive,
and speak their everlasting love,
directly to our souls.

And we will take our place with them,
in a cosy chair by the fireside,
and rest together forever,
in our new Rainbow home.

What of Dreams

What of Dreams,
a man's desires.
What of Dreams
do we make.
What of Dreams
that become nightmares.
What of Dreams
that are mistakes.
What of Dreams
that we never met.
What of Dreams
that help you through.
What of Dreams
that we forget.
What of Dreams
that might come true.

Songs of Solfeggio

Notes together,
a calling for joy,
or some melancholy,
depending upon your mood.

Special frequencies,
Solfeggio tones,
mystical notes dancing,
some high and some low.

Uplifting, inspiring,
bells chiming,
hearts beating,
over-crowded minds healing.

Soothing, spiritual,
relaxing and cleansing,
a delicate rebalancing,
of soul to soul nourishing.
Music is the food of life.

Sleep Evades

Sleep evades me,
sitting on the edge
of the precipice,
wanting to dive into the blackness,
wanting to be enveloped
into the silky caress
of no thought, no worry, no stress.
But still, it evades me,
teasing me in the distance,
ever waiting,
ever longing,
sleep.

The Night Echoes

The night echoes in the silence,
the merest glimmer of light peeps through.
Thoughts tumble through brain cells,
vibrant and cunning,
destroying any peace.

What darkness awaits me,
as I lay craving sleep,
the sound of the stillness
louder than fog horns,
of ships that pass in the night.

Raindrops start to fall,
a gentle whisper,
on the window pane,
lulling me to that secret place
where sleep can find me once again.

Beauty in the Darkness

There is a beauty in the darkness,
if you know where to look.
A soothing light for the soul,
as it repairs and resets in the dead of the night.
A secret life between worlds,
where our consciousness goes,
somewhere we cannot follow
except in our dreams.

New Dawn

A tired mind reviving,
the day after the night before,
emerging and arising,
the reopening of eyes and hope,
into a new dawn of light,
as you finally awoke.

Mirrored Image

I caught a quick glimpse of hope
in my mirror
as the person looking back at me
was a stronger image of my former self
and between my daydreams and reality
she brought me back
to where the sun smiles again.

Dark Oxygen

You were sent at the right time,
a perfect package from the heavens,
you sucked the dark oxygen
from my life,
the air finally cleared with clarity,
leaving me feeling as light as a feather,
all upbeat and cosy
and with the world at our feet,
you sprinkled me with fine stardust
and I was now complete.

Lovers Embrace

There is nothing
quite as sweet
as a lovers embrace,
like the silky caress of water,
in a warm delicious bath.

The touch of
hands upon hands,
lips upon lips,
ignites a fire that heats up a room
in the cold darkness of the night.

Once lit,
may the embers never die,
let love remain simmering away
waiting in the wings,
ready to be set on fire once again.

The First Time

In the stillness of the night,
I kissed a boy for the first time.
The sweetness,
lips locking,
mouth on fire,
with desire.
The passion,
almost maddening,
set to combust
with lust.
The lightning,
feels exciting,
hearts igniting,
with love.

I kissed a boy for the first time
and I really loved it!

Nostalgic Riptides

The waves carry me further away
on a cusp of nostalgic riptides.
That summer was so glorious,
the year we fell in and out of love.
You were the first boy
I gave all of myself to
but we both knew it wouldn't last.
I was no beauty school drop out,
and you were no streetwise jock with class.
We let the tide take us too far out to sea,
our love ran along the shore,
until it was not meant to be.
We hold the perfect memories
of a love now out of reach,
the riptides forever circling,
on our favourite stretch of beach.

Summers Balm

The lake glinted and sparkled
as the sun smiled down,
hands holding warm hands,
we stood watching
as paper boats bobbed along
merrily by the water's edge.
A mild gentle breeze caressed
a mere whisper in the balmy air,
children playing nearby
giggled mischievously
under the turquoise blue sky,
you looked into his eyes
and you knew a summer ahead
of temptations and suntan lines
had finally begun.

Smother me in Poetry

Smother me in poetry
tell me more of your love
a sonnet worthy of ecstasy
a sweet basket full of doves.

A pen put to paper
a rival put to bed
an ode from a lover
with starlight in his head.

A song from the rooftops
a lullaby that is true
a love that never ends
from the precious soul of you

So, smother me in endless poems
that feel more like sunbeams
and sweep me off my feet
with the words of all my dreams.

Marriage

Two hearts become one
lovers entwined.
Flowers that bend in the breeze,
twisted together forever.

Twin flames ignite,
the blaze intense.
Passion and progress
limb upon limb.

That which fate,
has drawn together.
destined to unite
Let no man divide.

Semper Mea (Always Mine)

In the beauty
of your elegant grace
in the beauty
of your fair face
semper mea

In the beauty
of your sweet essence
in the beauty
of your gentle presence
semper mea

In the beauty
of your tender embrace
in the beauty
of our endless days
semper mea

My Love

My love strikes a chord
with a cadence so deep
our heartbeats speak louder than words,
ever grateful for your steadfast care,
and the safety and warmth
of being wrapped in your arms.

My love for you grows ever deeper,
to endless moons and backs and back again,
there is nothing that can compare,
to sharing a life
of peaceful companionship
with you by my side, forever.

My love is boundless
and speaks to the night sky,
for you shine brightly like a star,
always guiding me back home,
where we can be together,
happy in our own little slice of heaven.
Thank you, my love.

Smooth Caress

Lay your head upon my cool chest
as waves of music wash over us
where we find peace in our warm embrace
and the heart still craves
its guilty pleasure
a flesh upon flesh
to be loved by you
is some kind of wonderful
and I now believe in miracles
from the touch of your smooth caress.

Is it Enough?

Is it enough this love that we share
to hold us together tightly?
Or will the dark night of our souls,
rip us apart at the seams,
jealousy, temptation, betrayal,
are all to contend with.
Will we be strong enough
to battle all three?

Steadfast Arms

Love is not all sunshine and roses
or stars that glitter,
or dancing and rainbows,
sometimes it is found in the pain and the suffering,
in the sickness rather than health,
in the loss and the grief
and in the arms that hold steadfast around you.

Heartbeat

Catch your breath
a whisper on the wind
a delicious peace descends
pulsing in union
a throbbing duet
enjoy this rare moment
of pureness
feeling alive
becoming one
as the heart beats
in time with your lover.

Young At Heart

Have we forgotten what it's like.
to have whispered sweet nothings in the ear?
To have a thirst for passion
and a raunchy love affair.

Dreams a distant memory,
the passing of time drifts by fast.
Only doctors and offspring tell you off,
once a certain age has past.

Aches and pains grow daily,
the body ravages along slow but sure.
Wrinkles and grey hairs multiply,
there is no magical cure.

If lucky, we have the memories,
to remind us of good times,
try staying young at heart,
just factor in more nap times!

Game of Hearts

The volatile tide of relationships,
with hope just a glimmer,
threats of a tearing apart,
like chaos theory simmer.

A heart set on high alert,
for the danger signals,
knowing the painfulness of damage,
causing hurt to come in ripples.

Why is love so hard to bear,
one minute beautiful beyond compare,
the next a world turned upside down,
with nothing but despair.

The danger starts,
when one pulls away,
to the find the grass rather than green
is several shades of grey.

Once trust is gone,
love is never the same,
the playing with hearts,
is a dangerous game.

Fracture of Love

The fracture of lover's rifts unmended,
leaves remnants of hearts torn apart at the seams,
tears wept upon pillows,
a deep sadness often unseen.
The pain felt in souls' sorrow,
often too hard to bear.
Wishing away the time,
until we no longer care.
A capsule of memories
buried deep down,
perpetually ticking away
to never be found.

Heartbreak

My heartbeat entombed,
will I ever be free of the betray
you left in your wake,
as my soul
turned from starshine
to dust
that day.

When Stars are too Bright

My heart was imprinted on you,
until the stars shone too brightly
and the sun wept in parting
and the haunting of heartbreak
became my new path.
You were my first love
and we danced in the rain
now nothing will ever be the same
and I must learn the new rules
for this heartbroken game.

The Broken Hearted

For the heart that weeps,
from loss of love,
know that I weep with you,
for all hearts in the universe
are intrinsically
joined together
and feel the same love,
the same pain,
the same loss.

When you cry
the cosmos cries alongside you
its distant galaxies
a weeping mass of emotion and
feelings carried in the stars.
Let the angels hold you for a while
and lighten your heavy burden
so the soul can heal from sorrow
and be free to love once more.

I promise you this
the sun will shine again one day,
the moon will watch over you,
and the stars will ignite for you
guiding your way,
as you take small steps
forwards towards the light
your spirit reignited
to let the love in once more.

Diamonds

They say Diamonds
are a girl's best friend,
but shouldn't it be
love, respect and honesty
on that we all depend.

Do we really need
a knight in shining armour
to whisk us off our feet?
When surely we can buy ourselves
the odd romantic treat.

Time to put yourself first
go create your own wildfires
wrapped in flowers
and exotic perfumes,
the scent of your desires.

Life of a Poem

Does a Poem need to be understood
or need to be very grand?
Does a Poem need to make sense
or seek to understand?

Does a Poem need to be long or short
or rhyme to be a poem?
Does a Poem need to have any meaning
or seek a life of its own?

Release the Words

Creative juices flowing,
like a river filled
with white washed foam,
tumbling round and round,
desperate for release.
Words upon words upon words,
crescendo and descendo,
screaming a torrent of abuse
like a waterfall of desire
overflowing with lava.
Until finally the climax
the consonants and vowels
crash together,
come together,
leap onto the page.
The story, the poem,
the book is done.
Is it 'The End?'
or is it just
'The Beginning?'

Sweet Morning

Sweet, ripened mornings glow
wrapped up in tender butterfly kisses
and rays of resplendent sun,
flowing with energy and vitality
as the birth of a new dawn is begun.
Each day brings a new treasure to open
and the stage is set for beauty beholden.

Spring Forward

Proud yellow Daffodils,
long limbed soldiers,
standing to attention,
Spring is in the air at last.

Sweet flutter by butterflies,
a floating paint by numbers,
of colourful dancing angels,
pirouetting in the gentle breeze.

The bumbling bumblebees,
filling up the honey pots,
working hard for a living,
with a veritable spring in their step.

Miss spotty dotty ladybird,
trying to find her way home,
landing on a child's hand
amid sweet squealing's of delight.

A brilliance of bluebells,
a carpet coloured cacophony,
the forest floor budding madly
as magic springs to life all around.

Choirs of angelic birds gather
feathered voices unite in the air
shouting out loudly together
Spring is here at last.

Winter Blanket

Cold Jack Frost,
takes a nip,
takes a bite,
takes a liberty.

The vicious hounds of winter,
reminds us we are
but very small,
in the grand scheme of weather.

Bitter winds howl with rage,
only rivalled by that of a toddler,
all red noses and cheeks,
with hands in cute mittens.

Winter sends us a message,
full of both cruelty and beauty,
when snow peacefully covers the land,
in its deathly warm blanket.

Lazy Summer Days

Enchanting flowers shine with delight,
petals glistening with dew,
a gentle caress of colourful finesse,
a day dawns anew.

Blackbirds are trilling
their unique song,
a garden awakening
where all belong.

The shimmering sun
guards over a bluebell sky,
clouds of cotton candy
go swirling by.

Sweet nectar awaits
the birds and the bees,
trees play a merry dance
in the gentle breeze.

Cats and Dogs snoring
lapping up the warm rays,
lawns being mowed
create a background haze.

Lazy gardens in summer
and all it relays,
reminds us of childhood
and the easier days.

Autumn Age

The hues of Autumn resplendent
a veritable kaleidoscope to begin,
the colours sadly fading away
to become more distant and thin.

Leaves tumbling and falling,
trees undressed bony and bare,
a lush carpet on the ground
branches naked as air.

Animals rush to nest homes,
away from danger and harm,
preparing hibernation cocoons
to keep them safe and calm.

The Autumn of our yesteryears
reminds us we are ever changing,
growing older with the passing of time,
our youth for wisdom exchanging.

Omnipotent Ocean

Only the Ocean can hold,
such opposing personalities
in its grasp
and get away with it.

A tranquil lucid beauty,
gently lapping around ankles,
as children paddle, shrieking
with innocent delight.

A terrifying horror
of towering waves,
tossing container ships about like apples,
bobbing ominously on halloween night.

An inky calm millpond,
which cruise ships glide slowly across,
like slumbering monolithic beasts
through the still moonlit night.

A stormy mass of seething monsters,
amid clamouring skyscraper waves,
seeking out troubled sailors
to torment, taunt and tease.

Only the Ocean
can be both
'Devil and Angel'
and get away with it.

Storm Clouds

The storm clouds wait patiently,
growing in darkness and density,
gathering more to the pack
like wolves as they hunt,
a clamouring of danger
brutally threatens every pore,
the hammer clash of thunder
and the laser sheet of lightning,
preys upon the scared in hiding,
as bedcovers become their chosen shield of war.

Seasonal Death Knells

Those somnolent days
remind us of years gone past,
when life felt peaceful
in languorous summer haze,
we long for more of those days.
Once blooming now fading,
the encapsulated rose buds
withered without care,
forever destined
to an endless cycle
of love, loss and despair,
as summer falls into Autumn.
Autumn time fading,
a death knell of falling petals,
marking the ending
but also the beginning,
as winter takes charge once more.

Sacred and potent,
black cold hearted moon,
as winter weaves her lune,
until once more undone.
She slowly fades out,
and spring is nearly sprung.
The promise of new life
from death abounds
and we head back towards
those somnolent sounds.

Only

Is a sunset only beautiful if someone is watching?
Is a rainbow only real after the rain?
Do stars only shine for the righteous?
Do hearts only bleed from the pain?

Do voices only sing when they are happy?
Do eyes only see when wide open?
Do souls only live when they are dying?
Is the world only healed when it's broken?

Full

Too Full.
Our cluttered minds
need space,
from the chaos
of life,
to help see things
more clearly again.

Unwritten Sands

Below the mystical desert sky,
walking barefoot on unwritten sands
the enchanted moon shines brightly,
as grains of time slip through our hands.
Beneath tranquil spills of light,
fireflies descendants of stars,
do their dance of delicate magic,
and shine upon true lovers hearts.

Tapestry

Life is a rich tapestry
full of ups and downs,
the worries,
the joys,
the too many frowns,
from getting on top of things
to hitting rock bottom,
one day may be perfect,
the next may be rotten,
don't worry be happy,
and don't let it matter,
it is what it is,
so Hakuna Matata!

Soul Searchers

All the Dreamers,
all the stargazers
all of the soul searchers,
just wanting to be seen and heard
in a world that's far too noisy
except maybe in the twilight hours,
when they find
all the right people,
all the right words
and all of the peace,
that they finally deserve.

The 3am Club

The 3am club
is not that exclusive
many souls
are on fire at this time.

The 3am club
opens its arms wide
and lets you know
you are very welcome here.

The 3am club
when the mind
is the most alive
with inspiring words needing a home.

The 3am club
helps you realise
what's important
and not impossible to achieve.

The 3am club
where tired souls gather
and find one another
in the darkness and at peace.

The Luxury of Time

What would you do
with the luxury of time
to do what you want
feel more in your prime.

More time to ponder
more time to rest
more time to plan
less time feeling stressed.

More time on your hands
less time on your feet
a feeling that life
is becoming complete.

No work to distract you
no feeling depressed
the luxury of time
would make you feel blessed.

Meant to Be

Don't let the dark rainbow
take over your sky
or let despair weaken you.
You are more than the colours
of an ashen night
that threatens to fill you with dread.
You are worth more than anyone
ever told you
of that you must hold onto and believe.
Once you open yourself
up to the light
you will be reborn
like a new baby
with few cares in the world
crying to be heard.
And the cries will turn to songs
worthy of beautiful angels
as they hold your hand
and let you soar to new heights
the strength in you growing
as you become who you were always meant to be.

Harness

Held at bay and shamed
locked down in chains,
my spirit was not meant to be tamed,
or hidden away in a gilded cage unseen,
so let the wild in me escape,
to harness a poet, a goddess, a queen!

Mirrors in my Mind

Mirrors in my mind
Seeking reflection
and introspection
hopefully no rejection
or condemnation
just appreciation
and innovation
mixed with motivation
and admiration
the mirrors in my mind
are mastering
my manifestation.

One Day at a Time

It only takes one second,
to be thankful you are still here.
It only takes one minute,
to hold someone most dear.
It only takes one hour,
to bake a tempting cake.
It only takes one morning,
a friend over tea to make.
It only takes one afternoon,
to read a gripping book.
It only takes one day at the beach
to walk on sand barefoot.
So, fill your life with simple goals,
forget the past and present,
one day at a time is all you need
for a life that is quite pleasant.

Soft Seams

The soft seams of life,
gently ebb and flow
along a meandering river
of trial and growth.
Telling ourselves
right from wrong,
being our own
harshest critics.
We hope for more,
we don't give up
and our hearts
gather more love,
to keep us going
along the seams of life
that slowly evolve
into the dreams of life.

Harmony

Walk gently through life
past the hustle and the bustle
love consciously
embrace the harmony
wear your heart on your sleeve
feel with passion
listen with grace
fall in love with this place.

Joy

Don't keep your joy
locked up too tight,
give it away freely
with all of your might.
Sprinkle a kind word,
light up a bright smile,
share out your happiness
every once in a while.
Let it out of the box,
unwrap and enjoy,
for joy is for living
and living needs joy.

This Path

This path you have,
that lays in front of you.
with its many complicated
twists and turns,
each is individual,
no two the same.
Your soul's unique journey
etched in the stars
and into the cosmos,
trying to find a purpose
to the truth of our existence
but what if the only true purpose
is just to live
as beautifully
and tenderly
as you can.

Each of us a Wonder

Each of us a wonder,
a precious star in the sky,
as individual as a snowflake
delicately floating by.
A beautifully cut diamond,
a single grain of sand,
we are unbelievable miracles
impossible to understand.
No two fingerprints match
and like a blossoming flower,
our precious souls reflect
a much higher mystical power.
The growth rings of a tree,
evolving minutes of each day,
each journey here on earth
as unique as our DNA

The Gift

Take this gift

wrap it up carefully
pass it on tenderly

the true meaning of life

is love.

Poetry Party

Coming late to the poetry party in life
and enjoying discovering words
I didn't know were in me.
Have they been sent by the cosmos
to find another eye that will see
or an ear that will listen?
Somehow that makes it all feel worthwhile,
knowing this journey is never alone,
for those who find solace
in the comfort of words.

Find a way Home

Poetry glides like the rising of the dawn
and the setting of the sun,
as they dance an infinite circle
of endless days and nights.
Just like the ebb and flow of the tides
and the constant pull of the watching moon,
the words in some kind of sublime order,
will always find their way home.

That Poem

In amongst the bad poems
there will be a good one
where the words flowed
in some kind of correct order
and it all made sense
and spoke to you
with a destiny and light
that inspired you
to go do great things.

It opened up your very soul
to prospects
not yet considered,
a new confidence found
to follow your dreams
all because of that poem
those words
in just the right order
for you.

The House of Poetry

A place where star crossed lovers meet
and ships that pass in the night at 3am
where stars collide
and beauty is found
in the constellations above
where demons and angels
fight mighty battles
watched over by the gods
where good overcomes evil
-or not
the inner most turmoil's
that transcend time and space
the bare bones of a poet's soul
laid out for all to see
that reside in the house of poetry.

About the Author

Valerie Fabian lives in Hampshire with her patient husband, intelligent daughters and 2 magical black cats.

Discovering Poetry later in life, she mixes traditional styles with modern and is bringing the world of Poetry to all.

Read more at https://www.instagram.com/poemsforpause/.